Perfect Woman

Jesse L. Stockard

Brilliant Books Literary
137 Forest Park Lane Thomasville
North Carolina 27360 USA

ISBN: 979-8-88945-247-8 (paperback)
ISBN: 979-8-88945-249-2 (hardback)
eISBN: 979-8-88945-248-5

Printed in the United States of America

**I want to thank
my Mom and Dad for their support and
assistance in publishing this book.
They both worked very hard on the
Photography and proofing the content.
Thank you both, for all you do in my life.
I Love you very much.**

Original photography by
Susan Stockard and Amara Stockard
Original poetry by Jesse Stockard

Other books by Jesse L. Stockard

LIFE
A poetic journey of the joys, excitement
and sadness we encounter, that mold us into
who we are and who we are becoming.

Introduction

In this day and time it is very difficult to say what or who is beautiful. The Media, Internet, and marketing campaigns shout their definitions from every roof top around. It's no wonder there are a lot of people confused about true beauty.

I have 3 daughters and 1 stepdaughter, all struggling with the thought, "am I pretty"

They have no problem finding their few flaws, but have great difficulty finding ANY beauty in them. This doesn't stop with the children, the mothers can also be placed in this category. I have no problem saying that most, if not all, society struggle with this same issue.

Beauty is in all ethnicities, cultures, and in every curve of every body. You see beauty is not about "perfect" it's about much, much more. If beauty was being perfect, then beauty would not be exciting, it would be the same as the next, very predictable, and boring.

Being beautiful is simply finding the beauty in the imperfections we all have. What makes untouched nature beautiful? The simple fact that it's untouched, nature is all imperfections, that's what makes it beautiful! People are no different, except we have personality, confidence, and passion. These enhance the beauty, the inner glow, and are an attractant to others. Have you heard the term "infectious personality"? This refers to the personality not the outer appearance, the confidence of who you are.

I have seen many women of all ages hiding from themselves in various ways: Baggie clothes, tattoos, piercings, strange hair, looks of defeat. I am not saying that all women who dress or look like this have this issue, but I will say I think most do!

I have also seen women who embrace who they are, and are very confident in their beauty. This truly is a beautiful thing!

I wrote a poem called "Perfect Woman" which inspired the writing of this book. This poem is broke down into 17 sections, each section has a photograph with a line from the main poem written on it. Within each of these sections are two additional poems written for that sections subject. The main poem "Perfect Woman" is written out at the end of this book.

Please take your time looking at the photography and reading each poem, you may want to read it a couple of times. There are many ways to interpret each poem as well as the photographs. I am hoping, when you read this book, you will lay it down with a new outlook on the reflection inside the mirror!

A place of impeccable beauty
View of mountains unflawed
Rivers flow fluently

JESSE L. STOCKARD

Sight Unseen

Eyes closed, breathe deep
Crisp air refreshes you
Your soul energized
Open wide, to an amazing view!

Mountain peaks, white, covered in snow
Sun reflects to you
Golden rays flood the valley
Vibrant colors of wild flowers
Hypnotize you

Powerful waterfalls gracefully fall, to rushing rivers below
Sparkling like diamonds, upon the valley floor
A sight unseen by so many, admired by a few
Nature's beauty glorified
Sadly ignored by you!

Jesse Stockard
12-09

City Life

Quiet runs, swiftly hides
Loneliness slips away, sighs
Voices charge into my sight
Lights in the city, oh so bright
People all around - singing, dancing surrounds
Neon streets attract my eyes
Fried foods," MMMM," my mouth cries
City streets full of life
Costumes, cameras, music, electrifies
Laughing, singing, yelling - so alive
Beauty of a city, imprinted in my mind
Exciting places, where life's defined
My heart jumps to the beat
My head spins in sweet delight
A joyous time I've had tonight
Beauty of city life
Truly, my delight!

Jesse Stockard
8/11

Wind blows softly
sets a mood

Storm

Swirling around a tree top
Gentle tugging, as it blows
Slowly gaining strength
Its intensity continually grows
Its voice is spoken, as limbs were broken
Squealing in the wind
Bowing from the pressure
Seeing how far it'll bend
Leaning on the forest
They help to defend
Angry wind presses, hoping to win
Display of power from beginning to end
Angry wind calms, gently blowing again
The tree sways, mocking the wind

Stay firm in your foundation
Hold fast against the wind
Standing strong together
Easily you'll win

Jesse Stockard
9/11

Daydream

A soft gentle caress wraps around
My head, my feet, my chest
This feeling of security
Melts my thoughts of uncertainties
Like a child in a mothers arms
I felt relaxed, safe, and calm!
Warmth upon my face
Awakes me from this embrace
The bright sun in my eyes
Blinds me from its surprise
On the patio, at the lake I stare
Refreshing summer breeze
Blows through my hair
Emotions of my dream engorge my soul
Wondering what meaning this may hold?
I know that God is in control
From dawn to dusk, young to old
Live your life to the best
In Gods hands you will rest!

Jesse Stockard
8/11

Where the bird's song sung, a sensuous sound crisp spring fragrance, sweeps the air

JESSE L. STOCKARD

Unheard Silence

Silence, a sound some rarely hear
Sound of the wind rushing near
Whispers of the trees
Turning of its leaves
Light to dark, is silence to sound
Things you'll hear, never thought were around
In light you'll see its complexity
In silence you'll hear its simplicity
Winds melody softly plays
Chorus of nature displays
Life's busy-ness pushed far away
A place of peace
Even if, just a day

Jesse Stockard
8/11

Sound Of Sight

Amongst the many are always a few
Seeking out silence, in solitude
Living in the midst, sleeping there too
Chaos – births – Chaos, what can we do
Silence's death, all around you
Explosions of life just passing thru
Silence gathers, hides in plain view
In the stillness of nowhere, it awaits for you
Birds in tune a melody played
The voices of nature, displayed
Sounds of water and rocks collide
This is the place chaos has died
Open your ears, hear with your eyes
The sound of sight, is silence's surprise
Fill your heart, discard your mind
Remember natures, nothing
Is most DIVINE

Jesse Stockard
10-13-2010

Stones positioned with precision and care

River

Lost
Standing in a valley
Distant trees
A lifetime away
It seems
Desolate, dry, dreary
Look ahead, look behind
North, I cannot find!
Sadness fills the valley
One drop to another
Pools become streams
Streams become a river
Soon a path arises!
Formed by stones, burying boulders!
Turning and twisting, lies, ahead
A direction seen from rocks, by tears!
Your path is shown thru impossibilities, and fears
Your unique path created
From your tears!

Jesse Stockard
10-15-2010

Friends

One placed beside another
A Friend for now, or there forever
Placed around us, for whenever
A time for one, or a time for none
There for a reason, if only a season
Some will last, some become past
All specifically set in our path
Giving, receiving
Making, breaking
All together their creating
Life's progression
In the making

Jesse Stockard
10-11

Beauty in its truest sense, could it be natures own confidence emulated there?

JESSE L. STOCKARD

Confidence

Confidence, is
Determined eyes seeing ahead
It's too far, some have said
Discouraging looks displayed

Confidence, sees
Directions clear
Some try to instill fear
Impossible for you, is what you hear

Confidence, makes
Distractions all disappear
On a course only you will steer
The end result kills the fear

Confidence, says
Destination will soon be here
A goal accomplished becomes clear
Confidence, is the spear!

Jesse Stockard
10-8-2010

Power

The power of a woman
Its prisoner – their soul
Sexy seduction, the weapon they hold
Aimed at the heart – every man knows
Allured, caught, the heart explodes
Love forms, emotions erupt
Evil heartless souls, stop from a touch
Blinders fall, from a whispers shot
Warm glance penetrates the heart
Loves astonishment transforms every part
The power of a woman identified
Weapons of love recognized
Confidence soon realized
Beauty's the weapon utilized
Open your eyes, authorize
Every woman's power is true
Reach in
Grab it
It's born in you

Jesse Stockard
9/11

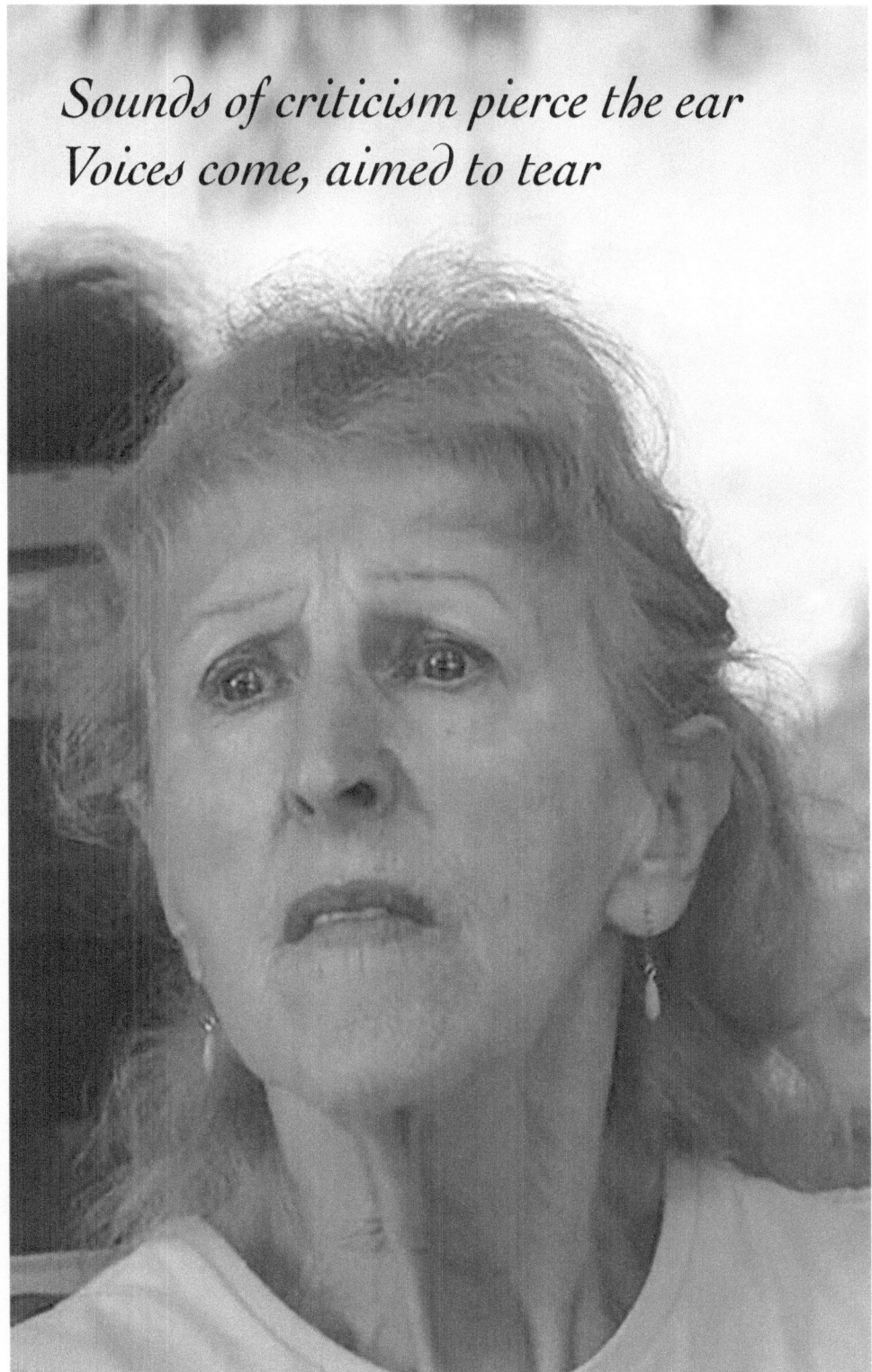

Sounds of criticism pierce the ear
Voices come, aimed to tear

Enough

Surrounding voices shout!
Worthless, Weak, Vocal arrows pierce me!

Evil eyes, full of lies, how they affect me?
Pain, Revenge, Depression rein

Oh! what do I see within?
Cold, Numb, Strange

Believing their words, what have I become?
A shell of where beauty once was
Now a corpse, full of filth standing in its place

ENOUGH!

Digging deep I will find
My true self buried inside
Seeing the me, I am suppose to be
Me loving Me so completely!

Jesse Stockard
8-16-10

No More

Quietly I sit, sadness falls from my eyes
Feelings of anger, fear, hate compromised
While love, excitement, freedom subside
From the inside out—to the outside in, emotions collide

Broken, bruised, scared, abused
Life with you is my issue
Success is like the blind staring at the moon
Accomplishment is to only survive you

Pain/Love means the same
To love you hurts, my bruises explain
What comes next, slap, push, pain
Bound by fear, chained by love, nothing to gain

Worthless my thoughts, failure's my view
I found my strength

I AM LEAVING YOU!!

Jesse Stockard
10-11-2010

Invective to others makes them immortal

JESSE L. STOCKARD

That Moment

Security and comfort around
A place that knows no frowns!
Smiling confidence abounds
Unafraid of what surrounds!

A moment that will never fade
The day of deaths parade!

Security, on the ground it lays
Convulsions of fear, each breath it sprays

Motionless all around
Safety to violence, smiles to frowns
Confidence, never again will be found!

Hiding in shadows looking down
        —I am—
Never wanting to be found!

Security an comfort nowhere around
This place, lives only frowns
Smiling confidence no longer abounds
Constant fear is all that surrounds!

Inspired by Kristine Sandt

Jesse Stockard
5-24-2010

Forging On

As my feet grow weak
I push on!

My head spills lies
Drowning my breath
I push on!

Hopes, dreams, promises explode
Melting life from my bones
I push on!

Words fall at my feet
Daggers sever my love
I push on!

Giving up, again, and again
To die is paradise
I push on!

Battle thickens, my eyes unable to see
My spirit cries in agony
I push on!

Tormented, tortured, paralyzed by accusations
Dissected by assumptions, a heart with a faint beat
Breaths a little at a time, I'm alive, but deaths my dream
And yet
I'll still push on!

Jesse Stockard
1/29/2011

Hard to grab
The lifeline we share

Lifeline

Anxious eyes, a fleeing heart
Finally out – a new life to start
Good job, nice car "OH MY" here we are
Bills come in — money goes out!

Our fragile path, soon cracks
Pressure, stress, no turning back
Through the ice, a drowning pool
Icy hearts, become so cruel!

A rope appears from the dark
Thrown from sweat –n—pain, hits the mark
Lifeline of love, can it be?

A rope braided from family's strength
Entwined with love, make no mistake
A rope as long as history makes
Tossed to us, for our life's sake
Painfully grabbing pulls us free!

Caring eyes, loving hearts
Wisdom, strength in every part
Limber leaves, tenacious trunks

Our lifeline you see
OUR FAMILY TREE

Jesse Stockard
5-27-2010

Strangers

Strangers are strangers until they meet
Side by side, seat by seat
Smiles flood the space between
Truly an unusual thing

Wheels are up and guards down
Slight hint of passion's found
Eyes tease a perfect view
How sweet it is next to you

Words laced with feelings combine
A stranger no longer we will find
Friendly smiles longing eyes
Moments to memories
A hearts surprise

Jesse Stockard
9/29/2010

Can't be slow
Faster, Faster
Speed, you must know

JESSE L. STOCKARD

========Speed>

10 minute mile to a 2 minute 10
A pace is set thinking to win
No trophy, No finish line
A race that will never end
Running hard, going fast
No attention paid
To the wonders you pass!

Eyes searching to win, blinded as you pass
Losing your love twice as fast
The faster you go, the slower you are
Never knowing the point that's too far

Winning, is seeing every moment as two
Growing life's passion as strolling thru
From a 2 minute 10 to a 10 minute mile
Winning is winning only with a smile!

Jesse Stockard
9/29/2010

One Step At A Time

A bump, a bruise, a brake
How much will it take?
A month, a year........ a wake
C'mon for Pete—Sake!
That love .... Only pain awaits
A blackened soul, a frozen heart
Run away, for its getting dark
As fleeing, blinders fall
Scales are swiftly removed
A place where freely, Love flows
DRINK, be refreshed
Journey of old, becomes new
Day by day, stride by stride
Eyes looking straight

Procrastinators are too late
Please don't hesitate!

Jesse Stockard
4-11

In this place be aware
Diffidence, is abundant there!

Words Of Promise

Sharp stabbing pains pierce your spine
Words fly at you, left then right
Emptiness follows behind
A void surrounds you, feelings numb
I see them, here they come!
Words of promise
Run! Run!

Deceptive in every way
They speak goodness, joy, and delight
Just to turn and stab you at night!
Beware don't be deceived
They try to enclose around you—n—me
Listening, believing, allows this to be
Suspicion, low expectations
will break US free!

Weatherly friends are who these be
Friends only, when in need
Oh, how I was deceived
Yes! Oh yes! I had friends like these
No more for me!
True friends are friends when they don't need to be
A real friend is one who likes me for me!

Jesse Stockard
11-09

Thank You/Your Welcome

Thank You!
A word of many meanings
Its meaning so complete
A simple Thank You
A complicated thing

You're Welcome!
A reply for only one
A reply so definite
A simple You're Welcome
A complicated thing

Words for one purpose
A purpose for those words
Meanings hide in such a simple thing
Courteous / sarcastic / honest / sincere
Take your pick
All are present here
Listen close
Depths of meaning
Come clear

Jesse stockard
7-21-2010

This war dwells
In women I know
Beauty defiled
Delusions adored

JESSE L. STOCKARD

Battle

From birth to death, we must go
A faint tremor to a MIGHTY ROAR
Weapons of ALL kinds in front and behind
All aimed to turn an twist our minds

Seeing perfection as faults
Defining fat from thin
True success as a major sin!
Media floods out lies, we listen to our demise!
How could anyone ever win?

A profile picture seen and judged
mindless curves, a flawless bust

-Lies I say-
A battle lost before it began!
Leave the prison you put yourself in
Ignore this war, let life begin!

Perfect is a view, One mind looking out from within
Am I too fat, or am I too thin?
No answer from out side-it must come from within!

Jesse stockard
5-24-2010

Victorious

Destructions intent is to destroy
Its arsenal it will deploy
From wicked lies
To mindless eyes

Its enemy is defined
With open eyes but a closed mind
Seeing beauty as despised
These lies grow uncompromised

This battle when fought, will be won
Seeing the truth, make lies undone
Open your mind to beauty's true view
An image birthed inside of you

Beauty lies in every crease
Every shape to every heart beat
Its view is pure and unique
Beauty is you, NOT in defeat

Jesse Stockard
10/11

Painting lines, covering curves
Can't let it show

Perfection Made

A canvas free, waiting to be
Ideas pictured inside of me

A perfect image, soon it'll be
Sketching it from memory

Drawing each line, painting each curve
Strokes of precision from every word

Perfectly placed, its intent remained
The canvas complete, perfection attained

Now, here on display
It hides in dismay

Perfection seen, but not relayed
The image is true, so why delay

Perfectly made in perfections way
Beauty, eloquently displayed!

Jesse Stockard
10/11

Shadow

Shadows attached to all I know
Runs just as fast as I go
Can't get away no matter what I know

Nowhere to run
Nowhere to hide
Mind and soul always collide

A constant reminder of what's inside
An image true that cannot hide
Attached to me its voice confide

False standards invade my mind
Thoughts bury treasures behind
Wealth beyond measure, within, one finds

With one soul and mind combined
Become the person who's buried inside
Embrace beauty
THE TRUE DESIGN

Jesse Stockard
10/11

*Through senses
Cannot be obtained*

JESSE L. STOCKARD

5 Senses

Bright City lights reach the sky,
    Stars and streets unknowingly collide
Silence so loud and yet no voice,
    Quiet chaos speaks its choice
Chills crawl up an down my spine,
    A caressing breeze consumes mine
Refreshing air becomes my breath,
    Deeply breathing fills my chest
Hints of life touching my tongue,
    Good, bad combines to one

Experiencing life thru senses God gave
Wonderful gifts we all can say

SEE yourself as others do—beauty has fallen upon you
HEAR your voice—a sweet sound from only you
FEEL the wind—intentionally caressing you
SMELL the flowers—sending sweet fragrance to you
TASTE the filling life that has been given to you

Take the good, toss the bad
Remember you, are the only you, people will ever have!

Jesse Stockard
9/29/2010

Power Of Touch

Often, I think of the power of touch
Pat on the back means so much
A fathers hug, felt so deep
Kiss on the forehead, a calming peace

In pain, a child cries, each tear caught
From a fathers hand, into each an every thought
Pain subsides, a fathers heart never dries
Soft, hard, are the same, fathers love uncompromised

Stern hand from Dad keeps us straight
A powerful love we can appreciate
Alone, in the dark, a father cries
When a child's angry words arise

Tiny arms wrap him tight
Peck on his cheek makes things right
A love so strong no words can speak
The power of touch is so unique!

Jesse Stockard
10-6-2010

All along hiding in their own soul
The way to perfection
This secret I know!

The Look

Across the room, my eyes gazed
Resting upon you, eyebrows raised
An image so clear, the crowd disappeared
Pounding in my chest, no breath to breathe
My body on fire, oh what could this be

I close my eyes in disbelief
A girl so pretty, not to far from me
Standing there trembling restlessly
I try to stop what's come over me

You turn your head and look
My body stops, paralyzed, your eyes calming me
Closer, closer your beauty gets
Who moved, it was unknown to me

This must be a dream!
Excitement rushed, realizing she is in front of me
Softly a voice speaks *"excuse me"*
I moved out of her way, she again says *"excuse me"*
As if she wants to talk to me!
Her soft voice again *"do you remember me?"*

Suddenly things came clear, *"yes, oh yes I remember you*
I was 7, on the playground at school
It was my first kiss, yours too".
Eruptions of emotions poured
I realized this was the love I was searching for

Jesse Stockard
10-09

Within

Afraid to look
Afraid to see
Afraid, just to be
Reflections untrue
Reflections fake
Reflections, a mystery makes
A voice from outside
A voice from within
This battle, who will win
The truth is present
The truth is true
The truth resides
Inside of you

Jesse stockard
9/11

Perfection an unreachable goal!

JESSE L. STOCKARD

Fruitless Search

The Search for the perfect mate
Looking high – looking low
As the self-inflicting curse continually grows
Satisfaction of this, nobody knows!
You believe a dream in your mind
The perfect one, someday you will find!

Realize, this one may have already come
Honest, faithful, realistically fun
Ying-Yang a principle that's true
Good / bad, both come to you!
Like a diamond, perfectly designed
Always imperfections, you will find!
Emotions, feelings, desires lie
With views of imperfections magnified!

Visions, to reality, we must come
Your perfect soul mate is
A strong connection, coupled with fun
A strong desire for both, to become one!
This decision is your choice to make
To travel the path of love through mistakes
Undoubtedly will make your perfect mate
Remember—thru pressure a diamond is made!

Jesse Stockard
8-16-10

Middle

An old woman sits, and waits to die
A new born, first breaths cry
Why the end, why the beginning
Seeking answers to the question, WHY?

The purpose for the middle, is what I ask
Why is there a first, when there's always a last?
Day to day searching, our never ending task
An answer to this question, difficult to grasp

A life for a purpose, A purpose for a life
A reason to live, A reason to die
Say hi to your neighbor, Smile at a stranger
Take their hand and rise to a new height

Try not to be hard and cruel
Go the extra mile, don't act a fool
Make a difference to those in need
The answer for you soon will be seen

Jesse Stockard
08/11

Perfect to one, not to you
A perfect woman
NO
Only a woman's perfect view

Beauty's View

Beauty's reflected in every mirror
A pretty face does always appear!
The viewer, the viewed an image true
Perfection reflected back to you!

A change by the eye, sadness brews
Tainted, distorted views from inside you!
Painful words of past is all you knew
Sight thru feelings haunt you!

Painful memories always scream
Beauty for you, seems like a dream!
Distracting clothes, removes you
True Beauty's hiding from view!

Learn to love yourself as seen
Share the love from which you dream
Show confidence, soon you will see
The most beautiful person, listening to me!

Jesse Stockard
7-30-2010

Truth

The view of beauty Confused
The thought of it, obscured
    Not the eyes
    Not the hair
    Not the thighs
    Not even bare
Its image is true
More than the echo from you
Our minds image hides the truth
Patiently it waits for you

We stare right at it, and can't caress
Confusing beauty for bodies
A religion practiced
Not professed

True beauty is not just seen
But a combination of many things
    A passionate attitude
    A selfless voice
    A heart full of purpose
    A since of Confidence
Innermost beauty, like a diamond should shine
Outsides just a canvas, showing Gods true design

Jesse Stockard
8/11

Ones confidence is all perfection spells
Personal acceptance never fails!

JESSE L. STOCKARD

New Beginning

Excitement, adventure is what I see
With my eyes wide open
The view of change astonishes me

From black-n-white
To color HD
What a difference it makes for me
Yes means yes and no, no
I like controlling me

A difficult decision I had to make
I see now, leaving was no mistake
A fresh start, new beginning
An unwritten book with a happy ending

Starting over sensibly
House, car, money
Oh yes! This is for me
Raising my kids, making new friends
This is just what I need
Me being Me so very happily

Jesse Stockard
11-09

Smile

Some think I'm high
Others think I'm stoned
People always wonder
When happiness is shown!

Is it wrong to be happy?
Is it wrong to smile?
What's wrong with laughing a while?

In unhappy places, frowns are born
Happy arrives where sad used to be
Bring a smile and see
A smile brings joy, most definitely

Soon a smile spreads
From me to all who surround
My happiness infects around me

Soon a happy smile is all I see!
From me to you, then you to me
Circle of happiness, you see
It starts with me!

Jesse Stockard
12-09

Perfect Woman

A place of impeccable beauty
View of mountains unflawed
Rivers flow fluently
Wind blows softly sets a mood
Where the bird's song sung, a sensuous sound
Crisp spring fragrance, sweeps the air
Stones positioned with precision and care?
Beauty in its truest sense
Could it be nature's own confidence
Emulated there?

Sounds of criticism pierce the ear
Voices come, aimed to tear
Invective to others makes them immortal
Hard to grab, the lifeline we share
Can't be slow
Faster, Faster
Speed, you must know
In this place be aware
Diffidence, is abundant there!

This war dwells, in women I know
Beauty defiled, delusions adored
Painting lines, covering curves, can't let it show
Through senses, cannot be obtained
All along hiding in their own soul
The way to perfection
This secret I know!
Perfection an unreachable goal!

Perfect to one, not to you
A perfect woman
NO
Only a woman's perfect view
Ones confidence is all perfection spells
Personal acceptance never fails!

Jesse stockard
2-09

www.ingramcontent.com/pod-product-compliance
Lightning Source LLC
Chambersburg PA
CBHW020342130626
46549CB00003B/1257